Whatever Happens to Puppies?

By BILL HALL

Pictures by VIRGINIA PARSONS

MERRIGOLD PRESS • NEW YORK

Whatever happens to all the puppies
that are born every day?

There are fat ones and thin ones. There are all shapes
and sizes and so many different colors.

When they are first born, you can see the puppies, but they can't see you—their eyes are still closed.

They squeak and squeal and feel their way to their mother, needing her milk.

And then one day, their eyes open and they look around at each other, at their mother, and—a little bit —at you. They blink in the light.

Now the puppies begin to crawl and play near their mother, nipping each other's tail. Sometimes they try to growl like big dogs, but what comes out is a squeal.

Their mother looks at them and wags her tail. She is happy with her new family. She has fed her puppies well, and they are bigger.

Now the puppies are ready to eat out of dishes as grown dogs do. Sometimes, at first, they may put their feet into the dish.

Some of the puppies like to shake a very old shoe and chew on it and growl at it as though it were a ferocious lion. Some of them want to sniff at everything, indoors and out.

At first, when they try to run fast, they trip over their own feet and do somersaults. The mother watches them to make sure they are all safe. But they are growing up. Soon they will be ready for new homes. Whatever happens to them then?

A boy and his father take a puppy to live in their home.
They name him Gyp.
An old lady takes one and calls him Bozo.
A young lady takes one and calls her Lulu.

A young man takes one and calls him Rex.
A girl and her mother take one and call her Emmy.

Gyp, Bozo, Emmy, Rex, and Lulu all live in new homes now. They are pets. Their big job is to please their masters and this is what they all try to do.

But sometimes puppies who have grown up just the same as Gyp, Bozo, Emmy, Rex, and Lulu are trained to do other special jobs as well.

Whatever happened to this puppy?

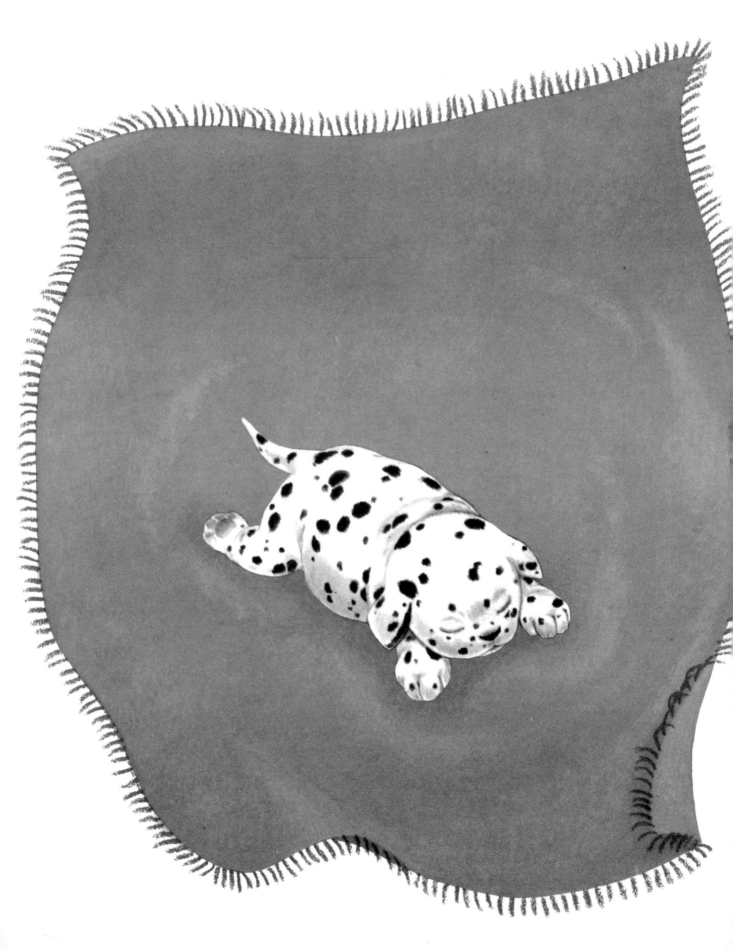

He rides on a fire engine with the firemen.

Whatever happened to this puppy?

He works on a farm, herding the sheep.

Whatever happened to these puppies?

They pull a sled across the snow.

Whatever happened to this puppy?

She works in a circus.

Whatever happens to puppies?

They grow up to be friends of man.

And helpers too.